Louisa Jones
Photography by Clive Nichols, Louisa Jones and Vincent Motte

Nicole de Vésian – Gardens
MODERN DESIGN IN PROVENCE

ACTES SUD

How could I or anyone else forget her? Such an individualist! That is rare and a treat when met.

CHRISTOPHER LLOYD to Louisa Jones,
personal letter, summer 1995

1978 I realized I might not become a good museum curator overnight, in spite of ten years spent studying art history at the University of Montpellier and the Sorbonne, the Art Institute and the Ecole du Louvre. I had always kept my drawing, theater work, costume design, as a kind of filigree threading through the rest. In those days, thirty years ago, it was still possible to change directions in this way, to listen to the voices inside, and decide one fine morning to follow another destiny.

Luckily I had willing friends, who, along with some fortuitous and decisive encounters, helped me forward; the openness and accessibility of some of the great icons of that hallowed circle, unapproachable nowadays, did the rest.

In short, in only a few months, destiny held out its hand and reshuffled the cards, and whisked me off to Hermès to become assistant to Nicole de Vésian, recently appointed as head of lifestyle design in her workshop in the rue de l'Elysée, now out of reach but in those days merely "out of this world".

Our days were measured by the changing of the guard as we worked in that parenthesis of English architecture, the New Vision studio, sheltered by the presidential palace, just steps away from the most Parisian neighborhood in the world. There I too fell into step. I had everything to learn. Nicole was unique, amazing, exciting.

This period will remain marked in the memory of future centuries by the disco and 'new money' look of the heroines of *Dynasty/Dallas*, with their padded shoulders, blow-dried hair and make-up.

Madame de Vésian was quite naturally just the opposite. If I recall correctly, she was both Provençal and Welsh, and she had the allure of a New Yorker with Native American blood. Like the 'Redskins' and her Mediterranean ancestors, she had craggy, weatherbeaten features, together with lively and formidable eyes. Her Anglo-Saxon roots and associations gave her a timeless quality, forever modern, with that inborn elegance of the 'less is more' variety, a functional style that made much from very little.

In those days, she also advised fabric specialists and decorators and our little workshop, in the basement of that grand building with its old-fashioned, wrought iron detailing, was a marriage of stone, brushed aluminium, brown leather and rough linen.

Page 4: La Louve's east entrance as it was around 1990.
Page 8: The lavender parterre at La Louve.

11

In fact, Nicole was the incarnation of the sublime illustrations of Galey & Lord, one of her American clients, those resolutely modern yet timeless girls, their high-chin style traced with a single brushstroke, that is not merely skillful but truly witty…

She had the knowledge and the power to transform her undoubtedly conservative background into a springboard for innovation, and a trying wartime experience of Spartan thrift into radical creativity.

She breathed in and communicated an *air du temps* that could never become dated, taking the word 'chic' to the limits of what it could mean then and no longer means today because it is less and less present, consigned to oblivion by the vulgarity of our times. It was chic however that represented the tenets of an irreplaceable (and never replaced) art of living that Nicole quickly transformed (her ability to predict changing tastes was not the least of her talents) into a new approach to the world and to life, both primitive and terribly progressive. Extremes always meet when this art is practiced with care and intelligence. I know no more Nicole de Vésians, except perhaps in deepest New York or the English countryside.

She used to arrive in the morning in her tiny car of the best green, loaded with canvas bags of her own design, dressed in a beige cashmere sweater (the motto of Elsie de Wolfe, "beige is my color", might have been hers, she went as far as only writing in pale brown felt pen). This, with a soft leather, vanilla-coloured skirt, just one or two Scandinavian jewels, abstractions in silver or gold, her white chignon impeccably drawn back to set off her tanned and weathered face with invisible make-up. A kind of epicenter of true luxury and seduction, with just what it takes of *hauteur* and bite to keep the picture from being too smooth or vapid.

A paradoxical encounter and an exchange of opposites: she was an aristocrat from the high spheres of rarefied air, I was a *petit bourgeois* from the south with flashy tastes.

Our collaboration did not last long, since I was seeking my own road, which I had lost sight of along the way. But my time at New Vision, working with this new and innovative visionary, acted like a crash course in style, a real shaking-up, for Nicole knew how to get you moving and helped you see what really mattered. She taught me what an endless multitude of tones could be contained in just beige and gray, colors that at first I thought boring, and all the little tricks that make things appear more natural, the apparent rigor of disorder, the right touch of the rustic needed to reach the *nec plus ultra* of urban elegance.

This woman who without her inexhaustible energy might have come to resemble a nun with Zen Buddhist inclinations, had already behind her a long history of inventing things and spurring on the discoveries of others. Was it not she, in anything but a minimalist spirit, who joined the elegant crowd at the races when war restrictions were still in force, wearing a hat made with her own hands out of a camembert box and a pastrycook's paper frill ? Surely then, in the mid 1940s, the height of 'contemporary'.

It was about the time I left that she began looking for the haven of her dreams in the Luberon. She found her first ruin, formerly a chapel or a garage or perhaps both, I don't remember. That was her first stop before La Louve. She cut her hair and her clothes became more country-style, almost maritime. I did not know her home at La Louve, by chance named after a she-wolf, so appropriate for this 'Mother Courage'.

But she no doubt applied to gardens the same sophistication as to her other apparitions, the same ideas, mad perhaps at first glance but invigorating, the same almost biblical search for basics, born from an art both contrived and earthy, a very civilized sense of the natural, which makes her places as wild as they are rigorous, with a *je-ne-sais-quoi* all her own, a consummate art of rules and her way of bending them to her will, an art that shows up the mundane as suddenly remarkable. Imperceptibly but surely, and with a fist of iron. Nothing sensational, nothing showy, nothing crowd-pleasing, just sound sense and innate elegance.

Only an aristocratic spirit like hers, free to the point of arrogance, could presume to match herself against Nature and the elements and expect to win the battle. Is she not today, in her chosen place of rest, the equal of what she so ardently cultivated, transfigured, reinvented, the very aromatics, stones and all the earth of the south? I did not know her at the end, much to my regret. I would so much like, today, to be able to visit her in her garden and learn still more…

CHRISTIAN LACROIX

Next page: La Louve, the kitchen terrace (2010)

A WOMAN

OF MANY PARTS

Nicole de Vésian (1916-1996) lived intensely several lives in succession: first as a resourceful young mother during the Second World War; next, for decades, as an internationally acclaimed stylist working mainly on Paris and New York; finally, starting at age seventy, as gardener in Provence. The impact of La Louve, her highly original garden, keeps growing on even in far-flung continents, where she continues to inspire both home gardeners and professionals. Although deeply rooted in the Mediterranean countryside of the Luberon hills, La Louve nonetheless exerts universal appeal. This amazing woman was called by all her village neighbors simply 'Nicole'. Today she is 'Nicole' for all her friends round the world.

THE WAR YEARS

Nicole de Vésian, born Llewellyn, was the daughter of a Parisian banker of Welsh origin. Her mother was from Avignon, in Provence. She was first brought up by an English nanny who instilled in her a strong sense of iron self-discipline, so much so that in her seventies, on crutches, Nicole climbed hills that gave pause to younger friends. Creative enthusiasm and curiosity always meant more to her than mere pain or discomfort.

In 1940, as a young mother with two toddlers in Paris, she participated in the ex-odus from the city when the German army arrived. She ran out of gas in the Bugey region south of Lyon, but managed to trade her car for a bicycle and a wheel of gruyere. She learned then a lesson that was to last her all her life: the resourcefulness or "make-do" that ensured survival, using whatever materials came to hand. She liked to reminisce about dressing her family with fur from rabbits she raised herself, shoes made from old Hermès purses, clothes cut from the lining of old curtains or her hus-band's dress uniform. She of course grew vegetables, and from her beets made sugar syrup for children's treats. Thanks to the bicycle, she got a job delivering mail. Alice B. Toklas and Gertrude Stein were on her route, and they all became friends. Nicole much admired Alice's ornate hats. She saw her first Picasso painting, a *Harlequin*, while eating Alice's spinach and raisins at their table. Christine Picasso was to become a good friend later on in Provence.

"It was the war that made me creative" she often said. "It was also the war that got me gardening. When you have nothing, you have to use your wits." Fifty years later in Provence, visiting the nursery of her friend Jean-Claude Appy, she noticed a pile of jute bags ready for disposal, claimed them and turned them into an evening dress, much admired just a few days later.

PARIS AND NEW YORK

In 1951, the Vésians settled in Auteuil in a 1920s house built to resemble a Roman villa, which they nicknamed the "Villa Pompei". Nicole's brilliant parties and receptions were much talked about in the press. She would arrange a center piece, for example, using bouquets of red cabbage draped with dimestore pearls. One Christmas in the late 1950s, she had an enormous fir tree shipped from Denmark and displayed it wrapped in cellophane, a material that had just been invented. The newspapers had a field day. Her son Hubert remembers this as one of her first efforts to use modern products. Little by little, friends asked her advice with

Nicole de Vésian in her garden in Auteuil.

their own projects. In the 1960s, she founded an advertising agency, Synergy, a subsidiary of Publicis, to advise clients on trends and packaging concepts.

In the heart of Paris, Nicole managed to find an abandoned coal depot close to the French presidential palace, where she set up her own agency, Nouvelle Vision, or New Vision for her growing American clientele. Christian Lacroix and Pascale Mussard were later on her assistants here. Her success was constantly cited in newspapers such as the *Sunday Times*, the *San Francisco Chronicle* and the *Christian Science Monitor*, where she was baptised the "career girl countess". In those years, she commuted weekly between Paris and New York. A fabric specialist, she became a consultant for the French Velvet syndicate and vice-president of the American Fashion Group in Paris. As of 1973, she consulted for Crompton-Velours, Burlington, Spring Mills, Galey & Lord, and in Italy and France for Ultra Suède. She created a whole fabric

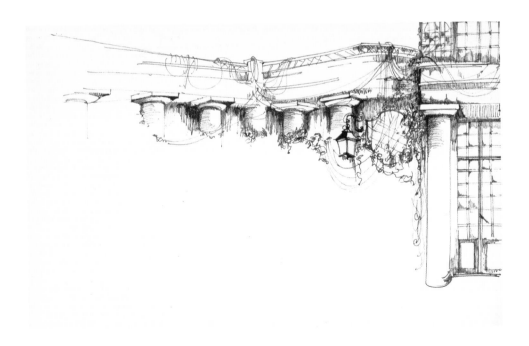

Notepaper designed by Nicole, showing the peristyle of the Roman Villa.

collection for Sonia Delaunay, shown at Artcurial in October 1977. In Italy, she worked with silk producers around Lake Como. Once, for the Bally shoe company, she spent six months studying their production techniques before beginning her design work. Nicole always sought to combine practicality and beauty. When the first household plastics appeared, she invented tablecloths that looked handwoven and even, for a time, had her own factory in Nice. A colleague remembers: "She belonged to the first wave of women stylists who totally changed our everyday lives. Real pioneers—the word 'stylist' was invented for them." Nicole summed up quite simply: "My job was to give everyday things distinctive style." Later on, when she had become a gardener, she went further and answered, when journalist Daniel Minassian called her a "stylist": "No, I am a creator."

She had simple tastes too: her cook left her because she preferred bread, cheese and a glass of wine to his elaborate lunches. In June 1963, she told a journalist from the *San Francisco Chronicle*: "I always avoid extravagance and expense." While she had a taste for humor and even at times provocation, she was serious about her independence. She told journalist Mac Griswold : "I have never belonged to anyone [...] if you are on a salary and you hear that your boss does not like red, then you must adapt your work to his taste. It's only by staying independent that I have been able to fight for my own idea of beauty."

The coal cellar studio and logo of New Vision.

Nonetheless, around the age of sixty, Nicole de Vésian began to work exclusively with Hermès where her mandate was, according to *Le Monde*, to "adapt classic chic to contemporary life". Here, Nicole first managed the ready-to-wear, soon bringing with her Christian Lacroix and Pascale Mussard, but later became director of the Art de vivre (Lifestyle) collections of the Rue Saint-Honoré store. Always practical, she preferred hammered pewter to silver, and mohair, which she found lighter to wear than cashmere. In one instance, she took inspiration from the tumblers used by soldiers in the trenches in 1914. Already a gardener, she designed a series of garden accessories. Always recycling, she later used bits of ostrich skin from the Hermès discard bins to line her crutches for greater comfort. It was then that she also custom-designed the interiors of five Renault 5 cars offered by the manufacturer to film and media

Pewter pieces designed by Nicole for Hermès, at La Louve.

stars Philippe Noiret, Jane Birkin, Marlène Jobert, Christine Ockrent and Isabelle Adjani. "We have a powerful relationship with her," explained the director, Jean-Louis Dumas, to a journalist in 1994, "She is the Hermès style incarnate." The Hermès archivist Nadine Vidal has kept a homage to Nicole de Vésian written soon after her death, which concludes: "Her creations and especially the spirit in which she worked are the perfect illustration of what was long the motto of Hermès: making useful things beautiful." She retired at age 69, in 1985, to live year round in Provence. She bought her house, La Louve, a year later.

NICOLE'S FIRST GARDENS

Nicole de Vésian remembered, as her first experience of a garden, stealing strawberries as a child at a family property in Normandy. Then came her war vegetable plot and the peristyle of the Roman villa where Nicole experimented, as she put it herself, with "a Provençal garden, unusual for Paris. I used to drive south and bring back cypresses, rosemary and thyme". At Hermès, on a roof opposite her office window, she planted a garden mixing globes of lavender and box. Her first efforts in the south were at Port Grimaud near Saint Tropez. In 1968 she fixed up a beach house (one of the first) as a stopover on trips between Paris and Milan. It was here that she began to prune severely so that her plants would survive drought and sea air during her long absences. She also mulched them with stones she collected herself from the beach. When she began to take longer breaks in the south, the Luberon was a natural choice. Her mother's cousins had property in the region and her children, back in the 1960s, explored these hills on horseback. Nicole's son, Hubert, had already bought for himself and his family "a few old stones in a wild valley between Bonnieux and Apt". Nicole's first home in Bonnieux was an old chapel already converted into a cinema and baptised "The Penitent". She later spoke of its "washerwoman's garden" of oleanders and red geraniums, which she gradually replaced with soft greys and greens, rejecting even white flowers as too glaring for the southern light. Much later, when the Italian couturier Valentino asked her to redesign his garden near Rome, she took him to task for his…red geraniums! In Bonnieux, the harsh winter of 1985 put an end to the colourful and banal exotics of the Penitent garden.

In 1986, Nicole de Vésian lost her husband. Her decision to live in the south was confirmed, and she settled in Bonnieux in her new house and garden.

LA LOUVE BEGINS

In Paris, Nicole de Vésian had already got to know Ione and Gilles Tézé, who later bought "Nogant", a house just outside Bonnieux. In the spring of 1986, Ione went to inspect a village property up for sale and invited her friend Nicole to come along. This was "La Louve", a ruin named after the last she-wolf of the region, supposedly killed there in 1957. Ione Tézé visited the whole property but Nicole got sidetracked by the stones, some

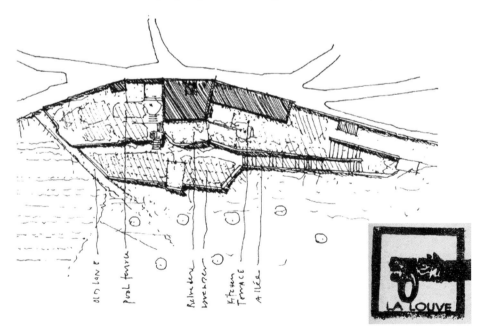

Layout and logo of La Louve.

octagonal, that she kept pulling out of the rubble. She came back later and even dug deep to find a lost well, flashlight in hand. Over the summer she negotiated the purchase. When Ione returned, she asked Nicole: "But did you ever visit the inside?" the answer was "No, but there are wonderful finds in the garden!" Nicole actively participated in the reconstruction, however, redesigning a house out of several remnants as she wanted it to be.

When it came to planting, Nicole de Vésian went to nurseryman Jean-Claude Appy who became a fast friend. At first, short of cash, she only took plants from the scrap heap, burned by the bad frosts of recent winters. This was the origin of her signature cypresses, their tops clipped square to encourage lateral growth. Creative recycling was always her watchword. La Louve always had a 'hospital' corner for nursing plants back to health.

Part of the garden of film director Ridley Scott, designed by Nicole de Vésian.

NICOLE'S OTHER GARDENS

In Bonnieux, Nicole once said, "I finally had time to devote myself to gardening. Little by little, people began to ask me to work on theirs as well. I told them I could only do this if I made believe their garden was my own, and also took into account everything surrounding the garden." Her first main project elsewhere was the medieval "Prieuré de Saint-Symphorien", once owned by Jane Fonda and Roger Vadim, then in the hands of Nicole's great friend Daniel Vial. Nicole helped him and his partner fix up their landscape garden, choosing which pines to keep, which to cut and where to plant more, designing steps and transitions, and even helping them organize parties. Many people remember

Gardens designed by Nicole for Monique and Jack Lang.

her being short of funds in those days. To help her out, her friends Scott Stover and Alain David Idoux engaged her professionally to advise on their own new garden at "La Chabaude". An American realtor working locally, Gwen Clarke, also recommended her to a recently arrived French couple whose garden, "Trabari", survives today. Thus Nicole began a new career as garden designer. Among her clients she could later count the film director Ridley Scott and France's then minister of culture, Jack Lang. She even designed gardens for her near neighbours at La Louve, to ensure continuity with her own. Little remains of her work on some projects such as the gardens at Bas Artème, although the people who owned it at that time took Nicole, along with Monsieur and Madame Appy, to visit gardens in England.

Nicole de Vésian's clients trusted her to an amazing degree. "She never provided any kind of plan" remembers one affectionately, "even though we paid out quite a bit!" Her humour was also appreciated. In one case, Nicole wanted to cut down a tree that spoiled her balance of dense plantings set off by empty space. A husband objected. She took a fine photograph of the tree and presented this to him, with the inscription "In memoriam". He gave in.

THE TEAM, FRIENDS AND FANS

Nicole lived year round at La Louve, working daily in the garden for hours on end. Early on, however, she enlisted helpers she termed her "team". She never had more than one gardener at a time, but these included José Bernard, a Spaniard with whom she conversed in patois, and Roger Jourdan, a former mechanic. Ghislaine Buisson, a young artist, became her secretary and friend. The "team" worked so well that when, at the end of her life, Nicole was invited to make gardens in both Japan and Italy, she accepted on condition that her "team" be invited also, all expenses paid. The clients agreed. Once asked by a film star for tea, Nicole arrived with her gardener, whom the star ignored. Nicole never went back. Working on site with masons, nurserymen, builders etc., however, Nicole could be tough. She never made plans but tried things out on the spot, getting the workmen to move rocks and trees until she was satisfied. But she could not work with people without helping them learn, and her many protégés remember her with affection and gratitude.

Two of these, Alain David Idoux and Marc Nucera, gained international reputations themselves, the first (unfortunately deceased when still very young) as a 'sculptor of landscapes' and the second, still thriving, as a tree sculptor. Nicole gave Marc his first camera, suggesting he take pictures from the treetops, but also that he draw his trees as stick figures, as children do, to bring out basic lines. Nucera today observes that both Vésian and Idoux, "had a way of working that was very much their own, very personal. They never applied a method by rote, but picked up their own sensations and sense of a place that they then put back in their designs. That was their magic and their strength."

José Bernard the Spanish gardener at work.

Nicole de Vésian, so much in the news, soon had many journalists on her doorstep and her interiors were widely published. The garden took a little longer. I first met her in 1989 when scouting for my first book, *Gardens in Provence*. The first pictures of La Louve's gardens appeared here, shot by Vincent Motte as well as myself. There were about a hundred gardens featured in that volume but every review singled out Nicole's. Many magazine features followed, and distinguished visitors. Film star Emmanuelle Béart gave Nicole much pleasure by saying, "This is the house I always dreamed of without knowing it." In 1992, I brought to La Louve Christopher Lloyd, Britain's most famous gardener at the time, as part of a visit organized by Michael and Margaret Likierman, who would later acquire the legendary "Les Colombières" gardens in Menton. With us was William Waterfield, a well-known garden owner also from Menton. None of us could

Christopher Lloyd talking to Nicole, with Louisa Jones and Margaret Likierman on the right (1992).
(picture by Michael Likierman.)

remotely imagine that La Louve would one day become his second home, when he later married Judy Pillsbury, who purchased the property from Nicole de Vésian just before her death (see below).

Groups of garden connoisseurs began to visit as of 1992. I brought the first, sent by Boxwood Tours, a specialized agency still thriving, directed by horticulturalist Sue MacDonald. This kind of visit soon increased even though, during Nicole's lifetime, they remained limited to personally recommended sources. Curiously, Nicole reorganized the whole garden as a result of this activity into a kind of closed circuit, visitors going down to the lower parts from the west terraces and returning on the east side. She also put in discreet hand rails by the steepest and most irregular steps, a comfort she had never needed herself.

In her last years, Nicole de Vésian had many Japanese visitors. First came actors from the No theater represented at the Avignon summer festival, then filmmaker and sculptor Higuchi Teshigahara and above all, the couturier Issey Miyake and his fabric director Makiko Minagawa. Issey Miyake later wrote: "Each time I go back to La Louve, I feel the strength of her spirit."

In 1994, *W magazine* in New York published an article on La Louve with, on the cover, the headline "France's Greatest Gardener". Nicole sent me this issue, marking the page with a sprig of lavender. Next to the cover blurb she added, with her usual irony, "Tout simplement" (no less!). In lavender coloured ink, naturally…

THE FINAL ADVENTURE

When she turned eighty, Nicole de Vésian confided to her friend Ione Tézé: "It is time to begin again, this garden no longer holds my interest." She suffered from osteoporosis (she had had seven pregnancies and numerous broken bones in car accidents) and so began imagining her garden, single storey house and wheelchair all at once. Hubert, her son, recalls: "Her last project at Les Blayons, on flat land at the top of the village, she had already nicknamed 'The Adventure'. It was completely new—a garden totally inspired by Japanese philosophy, with a house in

NICOLE DE VESIAN
née LLEWELLYN
1916-1996
MARTINE PICOT
1936 2005

The grave of Nicole de Vésian surrounded by the rugged hills she loved.

raw concrete, both organized around the needs of a handicapped occupant." The site, a vacant windswept lot covered with stones and ruins, unfortunately also hid truffles, so all the neighbors did their utmost to prevent the sale. Hubert remembers, "It was a major project and quite risky, since it depended financially entirely on the sale of La Louve. We signed together the purchase agreement for the land and were expecting to close the deal on the very day and hour of her funeral." Nicole and Hubert had chosen together the cemetery where she wished to be buried during one "cheerful weekend". The site is rustic, solitary ("not too snobbish", said Nicole) and has a stunning view.

The funeral was quiet and intimate, everyone throwing a lavender sprig on the coffin. This was the natural conclusion to a lifestyle that kept moving towards ever greater simplicity. Once established at La Louve, Nicole had begun to resemble her garden: hair pulled back tight, burnished face, clothes in rough linen

Nicole at work in her garden, caught by her friend Ghislaine Buisson.

or wool, perfumed only with lavender essence. Everyone admired her severe elegance, but this was also a woman who could, quite unselfconsciously and while talking and gesturing, lift her T-shirt to refasten the safety pin holding up her pants. She herself said: "The older I get, the more I move towards sobriety, restraint." Her greatest expression of this was in her garden.

The first meeting of Nicole and Judy Pillsbury (Henry Pillsbury with his back to the camera).

THE AMERICAN FRIEND

When Nicole de Vésian was consulted by Jack Lang, then French Minister of Culture, about new design in the Tuileries park in Paris, she wrote: "A garden is *always alive and moving*. Even historic restoration must provide structures that will evolve and take on flesh in the course of their lifetime." Nicole lived only ten years at La Louve, while Judith Pillsbury has owned the garden since 1996. At the time of purchase, Judith was a print dealer based in New York living much of the time in Paris. It was her friend, the gastronome Patricia Wells, who told her that La Louve was for sale. One visit by day, another by night sufficed: "I really thought it was a work of art, beyond anything I could myself create. I thought the idea of taking care of it and learning from it was a good challenge, a really positive project […] The first year I just watched the 'team', to see how they were used to taking care of it. It takes time to see where you like to sit, where the light seems really nice, what plants you become the most fond of, what plants you think could be replaced by something better. Before changing anything, I invited a friend who is a landscape architect, Douglas Reed, to walk through the garden with me and assign a quality to each of the terraces, so that even if we made changes, we were going to accentuate this original character. He knew this garden even before I bought it, as he had already been approached by many people wanting to make Vésian style gardens in Boston!"

Little by little the old "team" left–José retired, Ghislaine Buisson was replaced by photographer and neighbor Solange Brihat. Now that La Louve is listed at the Tourist Office in Bonnieux and has won the national label of "Jardin remarquable", numerous visitors are greeted either by Judith or, in her absence, by Solange. Two gardeners work mornings, five days a week, to keep the place tiptop: Mathieu de Bersac loves the shaping whereas Philippe Emelin understands organic management. It is Judith who must decide how the garden will evolve. Nicole was constantly trying new things, Judith does the same. She has greatly enriched the plant palette, adding rockery plants, grasses, bulbs, roses. She has experimented with euphorbias, peonies, hellebores, sarcococcas and the famous poppy, *Romneya*; she has planted groundcover hypericum, a fragrant osmanthus and a white moonvine. Her husband, William Waterfield, a famous botanist (see above), brings new treasures from his own historic garden in Menton. They feel that the kitchen terrace has best maintained the Vésian mood, judging from old photos. But even there the three central trees have grown huge and cast a lot more shade. Judith says: "I've let the volumes of things become larger because I like it that way. And of course I've added pots", something Nicole always avoided. The list of changes may seem impressive, but few new owners would have respected as much the original character of the garden. All those who see it are moved by it still.

A NEW CREATION

When a boundary wall fell down at the bottom of the garden, the neighbor decided to sell that strip of land, which he had always refused to Nicole, rather than pay for repairs. Here a true swimming pool was built, modern and different but carefully integrated as an extension of the lavender parterre. This was the creation of American architect Garrett Finney, winner of the Rome Prize in Architecture in 1994, designer of the interiors of spaceships for NASA in Houston. Finney took inspiration from the graphic fragmentation of the existing parterre and repeated these patterns with squares of zoysia, a lawn substitute springy to the step, alternating with tufts of pale pennisetum. Finney admires craftsmanship as much as high tech: along with his professional and technical training, he took time to train with a blacksmith and a mason. He appreciates at La Louve the "integration of the exceptional within the vernacular" which was Nicole's strongpoint. Nicole had restored the original rainwater reservoir, dug into the rock itself up against the house above, to make a dipping pool. Finney wanted his new pool invisible from the road opposite, or, if glimpsed, to be mistaken for a reservoir.

At the outset, Finney asked Judith: 'What do you want to DO in your garden?" She replied: "I want to cook with my children." Nicole was not a 'foodie'—friends recall that she cared a lot more about matching colors than flavors! Finney managed to hide a pizza oven in a discreet corner of the upper garden. In the house, he converted the mezzanine into a library, using pieces of wood found on the land and wrought iron he forged himself, cunningly adjustable. Garrett Finney feels, as Nicole did, that "taking the time to do things with care is not just a luxury but a necessity." Like her, he seeks to blend use and beauty. He too is fascinated by the whole idea of "change within continuum".

In 2011, La Louve will be sold once again and begin a new life.

The modern pool at La Louve designed by Garrett Finney.
Next page: Nicole showing her garden, around 1993.

It's great to be old. This is the best age. When the understanding sees clearly.
To give full value to the present moment

NOTEBOOK FROM HOSPITAL, 1991

How I would like to die...standing...in peace...
  in the sun...in my garden

  I love liberty
    Space
    Light
    Harmony
    Balance, sobriety
    Creative activity
    Having the time to make
    The time to read

  I hate falsity
    Pretention
    Excess
    Agitation

NOTEBOOK, 1994

NICOLE DE VÉSIAN

ART OF GARDENING

HOW PROJECTS TOOK SHAPE

Asked about her work methods, Nicole de Vésian liked to say with some pride: "I never measure, I never draw." She told a journalist friend: "I am very lucky in being able to imagine the finished project even as I start […] but for that to work, I need to sense the design logic, its balance and harmony. I never begin creating from a theme or a style. My approach is never intellectual but physical. Everything I do is physical." She hunted through magazines (clipping what she liked) and books (marked with post-its) for graphic ideas. Images of a door frame or of steps might be kept in reserve for use later on, whenever a suitable situation called for them, but each actual design emerged from her close observation of the particular site. For each, she selected a "jumping-off point" (using the English term), some striking feature of the surrounding landscape such as a cypress on the hillside opposite La Louve, or a group of cypresses already planted on the terraces

of the "Clos Pascal" gardens. From there she drew her imaginary lines, often a triangle, to establish the garden's "spine-bone" (still in her own brand of English!). Next she experimented with shapes, volumes, planes, full and empty spaces, suggested by and incorporating existing elements. In current jargon, her gardens were always "site-generated" and "site-determined", inspired by the character of each place, never the result of an abstract plan or some pre-established model to which everything was adjusted to fit.

She tried out many variations on the spot, constantly shifting trees ready for planting and even rocks from place to place. The owner of Trabari recalls: "She was obsessed with beauty. She changed the angle of that walkway three times, getting the cooperation of workmen who thought they knew what they were doing and had got it right from the start. I am always reluctant to ask them to do things over. But for her, and mind you she

1 and 2: Successive planes, leading the eye from near to far, at La Louve.
Pages 46-47: A house half hidden, giving onto the garden which embraces the landscape (1997).

was seventy-five at the time, they did it gladly, happy to be learning to see through her eyes. It is this rigor that makes her work so valuable." She did not only direct other people however: "Nicole made that terrace for us, stone by stone, she brought them herself from the hillside." Still at Trabari, Nicole had a wall built to screen the house from the driveway: "She wanted it to look just like the ruined walls nearby, using stone found on the property. But the stonemason, proud of his skills, wanted it perfect and spanking new! She stood over him and kept getting him to change this stone and that. This took a good month: every morning she was on the spot with this man, moving stones. Now it looks as if it has always been there."

Nicole's creative recycling also applied to plants, and not only at La Louve. The same owner had already herself, before consulting Nicole, made "a garden with plants like santolina, laurustinus, rosemaries, plants commonly found here. Nicole never threw anything away and certainly not a plant. When we started, she removed all of mine to a 'hospital' she set up on one of the terraces, and when the spaces were reshaped as she wanted them, we put them back according to her design." Nicole de Vésian also went hunting for plants in the wilder parts of the property, just as she did with stones. At Trabari, a grove of wild box on the lower slopes provided many seedlings. The owners, who keep busy with new projects, still use this resource. For them as for Nicole, this is not simply thrift but a way of maintaining a deep connection between the garden and its setting.

Nicole always imagined gardens in practical terms, not just for show: "I think that every garden should suit its place as well as the uses its owners plan to make of it. You need to observe how people live inside and out, where they want to sit to look at the view, or eat outdoors, invite friends for drinks or a picnic. There are never enough places to sit down and relax in a garden because most of them are made like luxury objects to be displayed, not to be lived in."

Left: Cypress trees burnt by frost, their tops pruned flat to encourage side growth, became a signature plant at La Louve. A graded view to admire over an aperitif at twilight.

HOUSE, GARDEN AND SETTING

Nicole de Vésian always sought to establish an essential harmony between house, garden and setting. Such was already the custom of the anonymous peasant builders in times past, as it was of certain modern architects like Frank Lloyd Wright. At La Louve, the house faces south-east, standing in the middle of the garden with its back to the street. It does not dominate the site, rather there is interpenetration: cellars are carved into the rock itself and the extension or "winter garden" has sliding doors so that it can open up entirely to the outside. The house walls link seamlessly with the drystone terracing on three levels. The garden's surface area of only three thousand square meters shades into the village above, into cultivated fields and the ravine below. Looking south-east, the valley is narrow and the wooded hillside close enough to make out details, but to the west, the terrain opens towards the distant Vaucluse plateau. Journalist Tania Compton

1: The large windows of the winter garden link indoors and out in all seasons.
2: The basement of the house at La Louve, built into the rock, converted into living space around 1994.

remarked in 1995: "The garden is really a homage to these hills. Nicole follows their contours in her clipping, and echoes their colours in her restricted palette."

House, garden and landscape are linked here much more deeply than with the conventional "outdoor room". Nicole was aware of a historic dimension: for centuries La Louve, on the very edge of town where the countryside begins, provided a secret escape passage for villagers under siege. In rebuilding, Nicole incorporated a vaulted passageway that prolongs the cobbled street outside and thus became the main entrance hall of La Louve. Instead of paving, it has a thick layer of river stones that can be cleaned simply by hosing down. The same surfacing reappears outside the garden door, crosses the kitchen terrace and rejoins the road down the hill. It is as if the village street were still running through the house and out through the garden. Nicole spoke of this

1: In 1994, the sumach of La Louve echoed the exact colour of a distant vineyard, which no longer exists.
2: The sumach in 2010.
Following pages: View on the west garden from the upper storey in 1989. The kitchen door with its "village street" of river stones.

as her "ruelle", connecting her interior to the very fabric of the village. At the same time, all the windows of La Louve were recut to frame particular views on the garden and hillside. The interiors flow out through the garden and into the landscape, a dynamic current that progresses in stages. Later on, when she designed the Clos Pascal gardens (with help from Alain David Idoux for the house), Nicole invented another "ruelle", crossing the garden diagonally from the entry gate to the avenue of linden trees at the bottom of the terraces.

By these spatial references to past history, Nicole connected the site's new life to the experience of previous generations. Today ecologists point out that human use of land in Mediterranean regions goes back some eight to ten thousand years, and that this "co-evolution" in its traditional forms, far from degrading the environment as was long thought, ultimately benefitted both human and other species. Such a heritage, instead of diametrically opposing culture and nature, human activity to natural wilderness, provides a model for partnership, a continuum from the completely spontaneous (un-worked) through the practical to the artistic. Each stage has its uses for human survival, each has its beauty. Thus the very same species Nicole loved (box, laurustinus, rosemary) grow wild on the hillsides where their leaves, flowers and roots were traditionally harvested for many uses. For farms and fields, the same plants were clipped into windbreaks and hedges; for parks and gardens, they were transformed into topiary or parterres. This continuum of human intervention has its exact equivalent in stone: from bare rock to sustaining walls and buildings, to carved stone, balustrades and sculpture. Water appears as streams and torrents, as cisterns, reservoirs and wells, as fountains and pools. Nicole de Vésian was very aware of this typically Mediterranean interpenetration of the human and the "wild". She advised using local species in the garden, and even juxtaposing very same ones (such as lavender) left free-form, lightly clipped or strongly shaped. Similarly she mixed rocky outcrops, stone constructions and carved objects. But she also loved to treat practical objects as works of art and stopped short of the elaborate. There are no topiary or statues in her gardens and fountains are rustic, like the simple stone washbasin by the kitchen where she rinsed off her salads. Old objects were re-cycled for new uses in a manner which paid homage to vernacular craftsmen. The constant alliance of stone and vegetation everywhere links house, garden and landscape in a manner echoing thousands of years of previous human experience on the land.

Page 56: The water reservoir converted into a dipping pool with its quince tree (1994).
Pages 58-59: "The village street" moving out towards the countryside; the water trough.
Pages 60-61: The garden, shaped and "wild".

THE LANDSCAPE GARDENS

In her early gardens, Nicole de Vésian often took the Luberon landscapes as her main subject. Today this region has become so fashionably associated with Parisian or jetset sophistication, that elsewhere the word 'luberonisation' has become pejorative. It was not the social networking however that attracted Nicole de Vésian to this region which she had known for decades, through family connections; but neither had she come seeking solitude in some romantic 'wilderness'. The Luberon, still today, is an ancient patchwork intermingling woods, crops and pastures, shaped by human beings for millennia. In her early landscape gardens Nicole had already planted clipped plant tapestries near houses, but her main focus was the mingling of meadow and woodland. First was the Prieuré de Saint-Symphorien near Bonnieux, a medieval domain belonging to her friend Daniel Vial. The priory stands

Pages 62-65: The landscape garden of the Prieuré de Saint-Symphorien in November 2010: holm and white oaks, mossy rocks, clipped wild box, viburnum and rosemary, with *Lonicera nitida* added; stone steps designed by Nicole.

on a rocky, wooded hillside overlooking the ruins of a village built in Roman times, vestiges that must have delighted Nicole. As for the trees, she simply thinned them out to open up perspectives, saving those with the most interesting growth habit and natural character. She clipped the wild box, and arranged or framed mossy rocks and stones. Some new parasol pines were added at strategic points. The whole site has been composed with scenes and moods that shift as you walk through it. The harmony of relations and proportions is so subtle that some of the neighbors still regret that Nicole never made a 'real' garden on this spot.

Nicole's first professional clients, apart from friends, were French, a couple of professors taking early retirement after a long stint in the U.S. They began by building a Californian ranch style house on a small plateau at Trabari, tucked behind a medieval village, with views on almost all sides. It has huge pictures windows: "Luminosity means a lot to me", says the owner, "and we wanted to be surrounded by all this beauty." Green and white oak and Aleppo pines had been long encroaching on crumbled dry stone terracing on this hillside that had once supported vineyards and a cherry orchard. Part of it had reverted to meadowland rich with spring flowers, still mown just once a year. Nicole first set out to 'edit' the existing landscape, to open up its distant views and frame its best features. She began with the house: a glass front door was put in opposite the picture windows to create crisscrossed perspectives indoors connecting with those outside. To the north, where the land slopes steeply down from the house, her main task was to thin the oak and pine woodland, keeping only the most beautiful trees, grouped into groves. The owners recall: "We walked through the woods with her and she said, 'that one goes, that one goes!' and marked them with string." The west slope, already more open, had beautiful multi-trunked holm oaks. Their tops were rounded to connect the tapestries behind with the cliffs beyond. All these views change constantly according to the angle of vision, weather and light.

The owners are happy: "What we wanted most was to keep the natural look…" This couple now lives here year round. They continue to develop new projects, many of which they do with their own hands: "Of course we keep on in the same spirit but it is Nicole who first determined the layout for us, the structure of the garden."

Left: At Trabari, the holm oak canopies in the foreground are pruned today by Philippe Lafoix; a graded view with perspectives on distant cliffs.

Nicole's last project, sometimes called "The Adventure" and sometimes just "Le Terrain", was to make a garden on flat land at the top of the village of Bonnieux. Even before the sale was concluded, she was moving stones and pruning the trunks of existing trees. Here as in her other landscape gardens, she carefully protected bits of exposed rock covered with lichens and mosses of different shapes and colors, and was learning to identify the rich range of wildflowers already thriving on the site. She had already planted some clumps of festuca that looked as if they had always been there. It was here that she wanted to experiment with her new sense of Japanese gardening but she did not have time…

Pages 68 and 70: At Trabari, the oaks were thinned, rocky outcrops shown off to best effect, and meadows encouraged.
Page 69: The "Terrain" or last "Adventure", only just begun.

What luck to live at a time when the notion of pleasure is experienced as a civilizing force.

Delicacy... that aristocracy of power. How they must lack it, those who call it weakness.

NOTEBOOK, 1994

SCALE AND PERSPECTIVE

The medieval hilltown of Bonnieux is sometimes called the "Mont-Saint-Michel of Provence" because of its triangular silhouette. Such sites intrigued Cézanne, Picasso and Le Corbusier by their asymmetrical piling up of cubes of buildings with layered roofs, alternating open and closed panoramas and graded views. The whole village is an enormous sculpture made of stone, earth and greenery. Every viewpoint—from above, within, across, below—gives a different reading. Bonnieux, because of fourteenth century ties with the papal court in Avignon, has the refined but still rustic air that pleased Nicole de Vésian. The Luberon is also a nature reserve with one of the highest levels of biodiversity in France, thanks to its patchwork of fields and vineyards, encroaching white and green oak woodland, cliffs, grottoes and ravines where dissenters found refuge for centuries. La Louve sits on the lower edge of the village,

1: Bonnieux village, a giant triangular sculpture.
2: La Louve was not designed to be admired from across the way.

3

where ramparts and kitchen gardens once merged with the wild hillside beyond. Within this tiny garden is a distillation of the vast landscape outside: a miniature field of lavender, fruit trees and many woodland species like those on the hillside opposite.

The Clos Pascal covers almost two acres. Its site is also a threshold, melding into the village and, below, into farmland and more recent constructions. Here as at La Louve, the blurred outer boundaries and the vague nature of some internal divisions make the garden seem much bigger than it is. However, each section keeps its own balance and proportions, big or small. The maintaining of harmony in diversity is even more difficult to achieve when angles of view are multiple and changing. Curiously, neither property is meant to be seen from the hillside opposite. There is no dominant axis nor hierarchy of spaces. Nicole de Vésian hated symmetry and had no interest

1: An intimate scene on La Louve's west terraces, with a thriving cardoon (1997).
2 and 3: Mirror effects at the Clos Pascal.
Page 76: At La Louve, close-up and distant views (ca 1994).
Page 77: By 2010, La Louve has become a shadier garden.

in what her gardens might look like from outside. All movement goes from the heart out to the world—to the extent that Nicole offered to help design the gardens of neighbors when they lay in her sightline. From inside the gardens, the overall design remains mysterious. Even the houses are unreadable, present mainly as a stretch of wall or the slope of a roof glimpsed here and there.

Nicole had an ingenious trick for multiplying angles of vision while blurring any reading of larger volumes: she placed small mirrors in the heart of the garden, hung at a height and an angle such that the viewer is not visible. Only the wider landscape is captured by the glass. The latter is always worn and tarnished, giving reflections a dream-like quality. Some are crisscrossed by strips of weathered wood to divide space and mask volume even further. It might be said of Nicole that she made no distinction between intimate and grand scale, since a whole landscape could thus be captured in a small mirror.

In her constant wish to link small and large, near and far, Nicole also developed a way of organizing views outwards in successive planes. Any garden on a steep hillside will have a panorama, often wider than 180°. In her early landscape gardens, she mostly arranged what was already there: sparse woodland, abandoned farmland invaded by pines and oaks mixing ruins and rocks. Here she pruned existing trees, adding or moving only a few, to open up long perspectives and frame a cliff or mountain. At La Louve as at the Clos Pascal, she planted a lot and modulated much more carefully the in-between spaces. She never 'borrowed' views in the Japanese manner, creating a sequence of framed pictures. Nor is this the panorama of a cinema screen or theater backdrop. It is rather a graded series of planes: shapes, volumes, colors and textures are set in overlapping harmony, leading the eye from close up to far away, first towards the hillside opposite, out onto the broader valley beyond. The effect is dynamic, even kinetic—some perspectives change as you walk (an effect taken up successfully by Alain David Idoux). There is nothing conceptual about this approach. Its effects are felt intuitively and with real sensuous pleasure.

Left and following: At Trabari, the new-old wall designed by Nicole with its successive planes, seen first from the steps of the house, then from the outside, approaching the house.

DESIGNING WITH TERRACING

Nicole often worked on steep hillsides built up by earlier generations into flat terraces, supported by long lines of drystone walls. On some sites, these had crumbled and become overgrown, while elsewhere they had been lovingly restored, as at La Louve and the Clos Pascal. Hillside terracing was first made by farmers using stones removed from their fields to create flat working surfaces, thus fighting erosion and making for easier cultivation. These vernacular constructions, unlike those stone terraces found in grand gardens in the Italian style, follow the natural contours of the site. No two levels have exactly the same size and shape. They are good for plants because they provide efficient wind protection and the stone retains the heat at night. Drainage ditches at their base must be maintained however or the walls will bulge and collapse—as happened at La Louve during a big storm in 1995.

1: Terraces at the Clos Pascal just below the medieval hilltown.
2: Paths in rough grass with apple cordons marking the lines.
3: At La Louve, rebuilding a collapsed terrace in 1995.

Terraced hillsides offer an exceptional blend of shelter and panorama. Designers must think of practical and visual transitions between levels: steps, of course, but also perspectives up, down and across. Outside edges can be hard to deal with. Overall, the long, narrow spaces created by terracing must not be readable from their entrance or no one will bother to explore them. At the Clos Pascal, Nicole de Vésian played with stone lines and the forms they create on a big scale: she included a whole vine-yard, a double avenue of olive trees, and a line of twenty-three linden trees running along the base of the hill. The top of the site can be reached either by several connect-ing flights of steps at each end or by using two ramps starting roughly in the middle of the linden avenue. Set opposite each other at diagonals to the path below, these slopes start from a small paved area with semi-circular benches. Each incline has its own character; one is in the shade, the other in the sun. This organization is yet another example of harmony without symmetry, combined with practical common sense.

In this her biggest garden, Nicole used some classic devices, such as planting small-er linden trees spaced further apart at the far end, to make the line seem longer. In all her gardens, she played on plunging views from one level to another. At La Louve, you look down on a miniature lavender field where she alternated rounded and foun-tain shapes, clipped and flowering plants. At the Clos Pascal, the whole garden can be glimpsed from the gardens of the Maison du Vin (wine centre) in the village perched high above.

At the Clos Pascal, which was long a popular village bistrot, not much had been done to the land and some fine trees remained: pines, olives, hackberries (*Celtis australis*) and robinias. Nicole chose to maintain here the varied character of local landscapes, mixing light woodland with vineyards and fruit trees, using this basic vocabulary to modulate traditional themes. Uninterrupted cross-perspectives occur only at the top and bottom of the hill, while the middle levels offer a mini-labyrinth, full of surprises. Each space has its own character, suggested by some existing element set off in the design. The contours of some terraces are emphasized by rows of espaliered trees or vines. The double row of olive trees is clipped into globes. No lines are really straight. There is no opposition here between the formal and the wild, for both are everywhere blended, along with natural geometries of field patterns. Many of the species present

are edible or food-producing. Many are pruned and shaped but many self-sowers like euphorbias, verbascums and poppies are also encouraged. Harmony here results from the constantly recurring presence of stone, plants and wood, along with the repetition of soft colors combined with rough textures. Strong contrasts evolve with the constantly changing balance of sun and shade. Benches everywhere invite gradual discovery, even looking backwards, a viewpoint often forgotten in gardens. The orchestration of theme and variation on this site is almost musical.

Pages 86-91: At the Clos Pascal, the linden avenue; the garden seen from the village above; a harmonious mix of clipped and free forms, intermingling *ager*, *saltus* and *silva*.
Pages 92-93: The lavender parterre at La Louve.

GLOBES AND TAPESTRIES

Mediterranean climate zones favour broadleaf evergreen plants that take well to re-peated clipping—box, bay laurel, laurustinus, lentisk, cypress etc. Many garden designers use these plants architecturally to create blocks, lines and parterres. Nicole de Vésian uses them sculpturally, allowing each individual plant to keep its own character. The results in her gardens cannot be called "topiary" since no preconceived shape is imposed from the outside and the natural growth habit is respected, even encouraged. Referring to the Prieuré de Saint-Symphorien, where she worked a lot in the under-growth of woodlands, Nicole said: "Nature shapes the plants into mounds already, I just help them along." At La Louve, shaping gives even more free rein to the imagination. Nicole explained that she did not want too much control but sought "harmonious patterns that still leave room for a touch of fancy."

1: Alternating clipped and fountain-shaped lavender at La Louve.
2: A planting that plays on harmonies of shapes, textures and tones in changing light.

In all her gardens, layered mounds and globes, grouped into three-dimensional tapestries, sit close to the house as foreground for distant horizons. Many are clipped, some are left free form. It looks easy, but imitators find that a fine eye is needed to judge proportions and balance, while allowing each individual plant to keep its own identity. Each has a different height, volume, tone and texture. Symmetry is rare. Yet the rapport among plants and between groupings and the setting is always harmonious. An admirer visiting La Louve once compared her plantings to a cocktail party where each guest is different but all enjoy being together. Nothing feels forced. Here pruning is not control but care. In fact, Nicole advised: "Don't hesitate to cut and trim—all plants love to know they are being cared for and they happily grow back."

1: Stone and rock plants at La Louve: *Cerastium* and wild bluebells against the house (1989).
2: Stone and aromatics: thyme, santolina, box, and *Choisya ternata*.
Pages 98-99: Shapes conversing happily together at Trabari.

Most of her plants are the very same species that grow spontaneously on nearby hillsides, such as juniper, bay laurel and laurustinus, myrtle, arbutus, and box. Some develop naturally rounded shapes into mounds and globes: rosemary, lavender, santolina and cistus. Others have a growth habit in the form of swords, like the iris, or fountains like the cardoons, while her apricot tree had been pruned into a goblet shape. Some plants change from season to season: the cardoon disappears altogether in summer. Nicole did not seek out rare varieties but was happy to grow easily available exotics, such as pittosporums. The square topped cypresses which became a Vésian signature were trees with frost-burnt tips that she got on sale. Curiously, she had no olive trees until her children gave her one for her eightieth birthday. A second one has since been added.

Such a garden requires little upkeep except for the pruning which today, at La Louve, begins in March, stops over the summer and starts again in autumn. Too much water or fertilizer kills plants like these, many of them aromatics, often shortlived in gardens. Judith Pillsbury has replaced the lavender parterre twice since 1996. All of the volumes in the tapestry plantings have increased quite a bit, which Judy prefers. The problem is to maintain a balance among individuals and with respect to the setting.

Nicole never planted lawn except at the Clos Pascal, where the owner wanted it for her children. Usually plants are set off or supported by stone—a rock, a wall or a gravel path. "Stones really move me", she once confided. She was said to collect them as other women do jewelry. Local farmers brought her their finds. Nicole always favoured samples that were shaped and mellowed, examples of some ancient craftsman's skill. Each stone, like many of her plants, had its own story.

Can Nicole's tapestries be called "formal"? Or "modern" in the architectural history sense? Even "mimimalist"? If "formal" means defining space by careful arrangement of volumes and planes, then these plantings are formal. But often this term also implies symmetry in the manner mistakenly called "French", where geometric design erases all individual variation. At La Louve, clipping is inspired by agricultural practice rather than by parks like Versailles. The pruning of vines and fruit trees does not make them uniform but helps them grow better. The results are graphic but asymmetrical, as in the work of modernists Thomas Church or Isamu Noguchi. Scott Stover, a friend and collector of minimalist art, feels that the term "minimalist" describes La Louve insofar as it evokes a process of elimination rather than accumulation.

SENSUOUS CHANGE

The conventional wisdom of garden history has it that clipped gardens must be cold and static. Some even attribute their formal shaping to the gardener's desire to dominate nature, at the very least to impose human order on an ever-changing natural process. In this approach, only free form, exuberantly floral gardens may be warm and welcoming. Is clipped greenery always cerebral, controlling and inert? In Mediterranean regions, movement and life are inseparable from light. According to her son, Hubert, Nicole de Vésian fell in love with the Luberon because of "its exceptional light, which here, at 500 meters above sea level, has extraordinary brilliance." Her secretary and friend for many years, Ghislaine Buisson, recalls that she used to go into the garden already at dawn to "watch it wake up and observe the evolving light

1: Sage, rosemary and common houseleek at La Louve.
2: Frost decked santolina (1997).
3: An almost black hollyhock (1997).
4: Winter light, winter tones (1997).

107

and shade before deciding on the day's activities. In the evening, after hours of work outdoors in this tough climate, she was happy to see the sun leave her garden. She felt the deep symbolism of its passage."

It is the light in these gardens, from hour to hour and season to season, that gives life and movement. Nicole knew which foliage types absorb light and which reflect it. Conventional historians also forget that Mediterranean greenery is usually aromatic, both in foliage and flower, concentrating its oils to preserve water during summer drought. For the same reason, it is often furry, leathery or spiney, tactile as well as scented, inviting to the touch and the palate. Nicole had 'an eye' but also a nose and sensitive fingers. Pruning aromatic plants is a sensuous act that liberates volatile fragrances. Nicole told British writer Mirabel Osler: "I am so attached to textures—very few

1: Summer colours with a touch of red and yellow (gaillardias, 1990).
2: Subtle and soft winter colours (1997).

people feel gardens." In one place at La Louve, two myrtle bushes are planted so close that when you pass between them, you cannot help but release their perfume.

All of these plants, even trimmed and shaped, evolve from month to month, in volume, texture and color. Many have new growth of a shade that contrasts strikingly with the old. Lavender tufts are green in spring, silver in high summer. Pruning here does not suppress growth but directs and accompanies it. The great English gardener Christopher Lloyd, after visiting La Louve in 1992, wrote "The garden's shapes show a bit of yeast-like fermentation and they are always changing."

As for other colors, Nicole preferred the tones of Braque to those of Cézanne, not to mention Van Gogh. She claimed she had once asked a nurseryman if he had any beige flowers! Shutters and garden furniture at La Louve were always a discreet pale blue or soft gray. Friends also claim that she hated red but she kept her self-sowing gaillardias and once scolded the local road mender for wanting to eliminate wild poppies from her driveway. La Louve is above all a foliage garden but Nicole welcomed self-sown, old-fashioned, cottage garden flowers: borage, false valerian and hollyhocks. At the end of her life, she got interested in the dark reds of certain hollyhocks and phormiums. Admirers sometimes forget that her soft minimalism did not exclude fancy nor even humor.

All of Nicole's gardens are caught up in the moment, in movement. Time is layered here, first by the many recycled objects, materials and even plants with a history, like the frost-burnt cypresses. Evidence of past use of the site is lovingly preserved—the cistern turned into a dipping pool, ivy roots embedded in a stone wall. There is also move-ment in the dynamic linking of close detailing to middle ground and distant horizons. Nicole de Vésian loved movement to the point of accepting disasters. When in 1995 a violent storm brought down the west-sustaining wall, instead of lamenting, Nicole simply started experimenting again. This is a garden where everything has a past, but continues to move forward. Judith Pillsbury explains her continuing fascination with La Louve: "When you describe the garden, it sounds very cold and formal, but what's delightful is this Alice in Wonderland quality. She had a sense of form and variety and allowed things to be different. Even though it's very controlled, she loved having wild things. Nicole was always changing her mind."

Left: Hollyhocks and lavender at La Louve (1997).
Pages 112-114: Twilight at La Louve and at Trabari.

The most important thing in creativity is independence. To be capable of changing completely, at any time...

The ability to see [...] different things according to the day—the light, the moment—and the ability to adapt them to my vision.

The ability to make forms, volumes, evolve...

NOTEBOOK, UNDATED

1   2

NICOLE AND THE JAPANESE

Certain admirers of Nicole de Vésian's garden art suggest that, having traveled to Japan as a stylist, she took direct inspiration from Japanese gardens when she created La Louve. The evidence does not bear this out: in the many in-depth interviews about La Louve that she gave between 1989 and 1995, Nicole never mentioned Japan. Nor were any of her knowledgeable visitors during this period struck by similarities. Like Nicole herself, they all comment on her local inspiration—the shapes, textures, tones and light of the Luberon hills. Japan is only mentioned after 1995, when Nicole first received Japanese visitors. At that time, she definitely got seriously interested in Japanese gardens. I myself gave her that year a copy of Tanizaki's *In Praise of Shadow*. When she died in 1996, she was planning a new garden under Japanese influence, and she had been invited to make a garden in Japan.

Hand-crafted stonework at La Louve: a bench designed by Nicole (1); a found stone globe on a drystone column (2), and dead ivy roots turned into land art (3).

After her passing, the reputation of La Louve kept growing. Two serious historians, John Brookes and Penelope Hill, praised it in 1997 and 1998, again with no mention of Asian inspiration. It is in Paris, as of 2000, that this connection first appears, when a journalist evokes "compositions in the Japanese mode." Jean-Paul Pigeat in his book on Japanese gardens speaks of "convergence" rather than influence. Today a cosmopolitan public, often more familiar with Kyoto than with Provence, just assumes Japanese inspiration, perhaps because the Asian link is felt to confer prestige on a garden created in a region—Provence—often deemed of mere holiday interest.

Visitors cite the presence of rock and stone, clipped shrubs and carefully framed views as at least echoing, if not directly inspired by, Japanese gardens. The similarities are superficial, however. The stones treasured by Nicole de Vésian were not rough specimens found in the wild but rustic, domestic objects, valued all the more for having been shaped by human hands. The pruning of trees in both Provence and Japan follows natural growth habit. In Japan, however, it is part of a symbolic reduction that peaks in the art of bonsai. Japan has a moist climate where clipped contours catch wisps of mist, raindrops, and moonlight. La Louve is a particularly dry and sunstruck garden, where shapes are sharp and crisp, the light brilliant. As for views beyond, there are many ways to link landscapes and gardens. In Japan, windows in walls or hedging provide pictures in carefully framed sequence, planned for a single viewpoint. At La Louve, perspectives are multiple and crisscrossing, and meant to change as you walk. There are other important differences: gardening in Japan is an elite art, imperial, aristocratic or sacred, still rarely accessible to women. Above all perhaps, the Japanese insist that their gardens are an abstraction from nature, not an imitation. Whereas Nicole enjoyed manual work, mistrusted abstraction and took her inspiration rather from peasant or vernacular traditions.

And yet…in her last years, Nicole de Vésian was about to make a 'Japanese' garden. What affinities did she feel? Judith Pillsbury, who took over La Louve at Nicole's death, found in Nicole's library a precious book, *A Japanese Touch for Your Garden*, annotated by Nicole. The following passages were marked: "In a garden in a small enclosed area, the gardener does not fill it up, this would only congest it. Instead he carefully arranges a few items and uses their relationships to suggest more than is immediately visible to the eye"; "He aims for balance and proportion without resorting to geometric artifice. He links the garden compositionally to his home, and he exploits

Recently created, Japanese-inspired shapes by sculptor Marc Nucera at La Louve.

numerous untouchables, wind directions, sound, seasons, sunlight, the true and apparent dimensions of empty space." Or again, "The Japanese gardener shapes his trees to expose their true qualities and to give them a balanced form that harmonizes with the rest of the garden. Most tree configurations are derived from actual examples seen in areas that are well exposed to the elements such as a seashore or mountain top." Here Nicole made a marginal notation "Holm oaks". She also marked: "Within a hard stone are movement, direction, centuries of accumulated time. The gardener's task is to make these qualities visible to the human eye." Here there is obvious convergence…

Pages 120 to 125: At La Louve, the sun creates strong contrasts between bright and shaded zones. The landscape beyond is not so much "borrowed" as an integral part of the garden throughout. But the plants here are gently and sometimes playfully shaped, as in Japan.

1

2

NICOLE AND THE MEDITERRANEAN

Nicole de Vésian chose to restore a simple village property with little land, neither chateau nor bastide. She made no attempt to gentrify it by adding greater symmetry or sculpted detailing. "This is not a rich person's garden" she often said, with some pride. Yet she did not fall into pastoral pastiche. She had always loved modern materials; the rough concrete beams of her winter garden remain clearly visible. In the old as well as in the new, she valued simplicity. She who designed interior objects for Hermès could compose a still life on her patio table with just a simple plate of cherries or a pumpkin sitting on fig leaves. Even rusty barrel hoops hung on a peg where they cast moving shadows on the stone behind them were a sculpture for Nicole de Vésian. She did not like the contrived look of plants in pots, nor the frequent watering they require. But she collected baskets and hats, objects that are useful, decorative and mobile.

1: La Louve: weeding basket (1990).
2 and 3: Domestic still lifes by Vésian: pumpkin, grapes and fig leaves; barrel hoops on a peg (1994-1996).

Nicole told the journalist Daniel Minassian: "I like to create on roots. I like things to be logical but also part of everyday life. I hate pretention, gratuity. I am close to the earth, I have my feet on the ground, I want everything I create to be practical, logical, rational—an ideal not far removed from good design. There is no reason things can't be both practical and beautiful." Vernacular art is often discounted because its aims are utilitarian rather than aesthetic. Nicole fought all her life against the separation of use and beauty as against the distinction between art and craft, or head and hand. She knew, from her war years, that necessity is the mother of invention. She was above all sensitive not only to spirit but to the logic of place, the need governing most choices in building and planting in traditional countrysides, to harmonize with the climate and setting.

1 and 2: At La Louve, elements from of the rural past (mainly in stone) have been recycled.
Page 130: One of the "bories" (stone huts) at Trabari.
Page 131: Vines growing on the upper terrace of the Clos Pascal.

Conventional garden historians usually separate productive from ornamental gardening, a split that does not work in the Mediterranean. Are the lavenders Nicole loved to the point of wearing fragrance distilled from their flowers decorative or productive? She planted near them an apricot tree which she appreciated for its shape, its bark, the changing color of its young leaves and the taste of its fruit—useful or beautiful? In a similar spirit, she loved all seasons, some bringing flowers, some bringing fruit. The current owner conducts a ceremony of wrapping plants in the Japanese mode for the winter when, for her, the garden's life has stopped. Nicole sometimes said she loved her garden best in the winter light, with a sky cleared by a blast of mistral wind, when it is often possible to lunch outdoors, and when the best new ideas are hatched.

Nicole de Vésian once advised her friend Frankie Coxe of the Carmejane gardens in Ménerbes: "Learn to listen to the land." In Provence, landscapes were originally organized by Roman surveyors into a mix of *ager*, *saltus* and *silva* (fields, pasture and woodland). Nicole took inspiration from this patchwork, still common today in the Luberon. A scrapbook she gave to the owners of La Chabaude shows how a project for a lavender parterre in a herringbone pattern was inspired by two vineyards juxtaposed on a hilltop. She liked to include vestiges of the rustic past in all of her gardens: drystone terracing, steps, paths and walls, irrigation ditches, water reservoirs. She recognized the Mediterranean landscapes as a palimpsest (a manuscript written on over and over again), each generation adding its experience to the last. Even in pruning, she adapted ancestral gestures to new needs and uses. Her whole art of gardening was a sort of cultural recycling of the peasant past, where economy of resources was put to ingenious use in conditions that were often austere. The American designer Garrett Finney, when he worked himself at La Louve, praised Nicole for her "integration of the exceptional within the vernacular" and her sense of "change in continuum". A historian of vernacular architecture, Victor Papanek, judges that these structures, "human in scale", possess "a sensual frugality that results in true elegance". These last words summarize beautifully the art of Nicole de Vésian.

Left: At La Louve: the lavender field and flowering apricot tree (1997).
Pages 134-135: The garden unfolding towards the landscape (2010).
Page 136: A young garden, as it was in 1989.
Pages 138-139: The same scene, in 2010.

Television just kills me. The nearest cinema is fifty kilometres away. I don't see why I should go see a show when I have such an amazing display right here, every day. These infinite, barely perceptible changes of the earth are far more precious to me.

PERSONAL LETTER, 1996

AND STILL MORE...

Don't hesitate to cut and trim—all plants love to know they are being cared for and they happily grow back.

Gather stones, using them for borders, to frame and protect the plants from the cold or the sun.

Look for all the plants that grow wild in your area and adopt them for your garden.

Remember the sense of smell in a garden—use lavender, rosemary, sage, thyme or mint for subtle fragrances.

Use herbs as sensible borders for walkways.

Make a narrow path between two rows of boxtree or myrtle to create an exquisitely scented passage that comes alive as you pass through.

Use a chair to sit in a garden when planning, taking in all the views—a garden should be seen seated.

Think multi-dimensionally—a garden is not just a grid, it should be seen in diagonals and thought of in terms of floors or levels.

Play with different ways of trimming the same kind of plant (cut very short, cut slightly, and wild)—the alternating textures create interest.

Frame the view—trees, plants and arches should be used to put the view in perspective.

AS PUBLISHED IN *W MAGAZINE*, 1994

Left: Steps leading to the swimming-pool at the Clos Pascal (1997).

PLANTS AT LA LOUVE:
A WELL-STOCKED AND CLEVER GARDEN

Nicole de Vésian, and later Judith Pillsbury, created this iconic and innovative garden, far richer in its plant content than appears at first glance. Its overall harmony makes us lose sight of the diversity of species present.

TREES:

Among the trees which stand facing the Luberon hills, framing the views, and holding up the sky:

Abies pinsapo: Spanish fir, common in the sierras, especially in Nevada, was introduced into the Luberon region by the forestry services and local nurseries in the 1950s and 1960s.

Almond: So typical of the backways and byways of Provence, white and pink flowering, graceful, a promise of spring sometimes premature…

Arbutus unedo: The arbutus or strawberry tree which bears fruit and its lily-of-the-valley type flowers together in late autumn and winter; its strong green foliage is set off by the nuances of gray and silver surrounding it.

Celtis australis: The hackberry or nettle tree, long trained to produce pitchforks, bronze-green foliage, mouse-gray bark, an elegant silhouette rising behind a hedge.

Cercis siliquastrum: The Judas tree, first big explosion of pink in spring on black branches, before the leaves appear (how could Judas have ever hung himself on these branches, too fragile and too beautiful for such remorse!)

Cupressus arizonica fastigiata glauca: The blue cypress used for hedging everywhere in sprawling, post-war housing developments, so exasperating in the monotony of its blue-gray tones, decimated by a species-linked, sap-sucking parasite (the *Cinara cupressi*), so much so that it has now disappeared from our gardens. And yet Nicole recycled it, integrated it, grew it well, set off in isolation its peeling bark and its noble growth habit which echo its origins, the Rocky Mountains!

Cupressus sempervirens: The cypress of Provence or Tuscany; from a dying reject restored to life, Nicole made a rocket in the sky.

Eriobotrya japonica: The Japanese loquat, evergreen, with perfumed flowers in November and December. Its fruit is often frozen before it is ripe in the Luberon region. But it is an exotic tree often found with the jujube tree in old Provençal farms.

Fig: Everywhere present, symbol of fertility, the delight of insects and of all Mediterraneans.

Lagerstroemia indica: Indian or summer lilac, recently introduced, with clusters of pink or red flowers. At La Louve it contrasts with the rigor of other plantings, an example of Nicole's ability to create contrasts, here for late summer.

Taxus baccata: The yew with its poison berries and ever dark needles, must originally have come to La Louve from a nursery, long before Nicole's time. It lends itself to every kind of clipping. The two enormous specimens at La Louve were broken in half by the storm of 1995 and remain as two giant dark-green cartwheels on the edge of the west terrace.

TWO CLIMBERS:

Rosa banksia: The "Lady Banks" rose, which has found its place on many pergolas and trellises in Provence, here sends out its little white or yellow roses to conquer walls and trees, a quickly passing explosion in equally fleeting April.

Polygonum aubertii: Japanese knotweed with its little there are can be invasive but is very practical for filling up bare spaces and covering ugly piles of rubble.

SHRUBS:

Among the many shrubs pruned in a thousand ways, there are bursts of floral color carefully placed among the mounds and squared off beds. All were either found in the wild or chosen with the generous advice of nurserymen who were among Nicole's greatest admirers.

Lending themselves to shaping:

Pineapple guava (*Acca sellowiana*), *Atriplex halimus*, boxwood (all the European varieties are present in this garden), evergreen eleagnus (*Eleagnus ebbingei*), spindle tree (*Euonymus europaeus*), *Lonicera nitida*, myrtle (*Myrtus tarentina*, the only hardy one for backcountry Provence), *Myrsina africana*, the Asian pittosporums (*P. tenuifolium* and *P. tobira nana*), shrubby germander (*Teucrium fruticans*), Mexican orange (*Choisya ternata*), laurustinus (*Viburnum tinus*) which is a great classic for topiary as well as a wild plant in Provence. Without forgetting filaria (*Phillyrea angustifolia* and *latifolia* or *media*), a plant recovered for gardens from the scrubland of Provence first by my own family nursery, though already used by the Romans, extraordinary in its resistance to cold, heat, drought, floods and the strongest pruning. Unclipped, left to flower: the cistus, notably *Cistus* x *sunset*, and *C.* x *purpureus*) and the Mexican orange. For contrasting shapes, *Yucca aloifolia* with its sharp sword leaves and the humble domestic cardoon.

Colorful accents, often fragrant, flowering throughout the year:

Japanese quince, coronilla, the Australian *Grevillea rosmarinifolia*, the hibiscus or mallow tree, the mock orange or syringa of our grandmothers, two China roses (*Rosa sanguinea* and *mutabilis*), bergenias, false valerian (*Centranthus ruber*), wallflowers, sweet William, euphorbias, perennial geraniums, Corsican hellebores and Christmas roses. And of course her legendary lavenders: at low altitude (as at Bonnieux) the best cultivars are the 'Grosso', 'Seguret', 'Jaubert', etc., and the lavandin, hybrid of the high altitude true lavender (*Lavandula vera*) and of the lower, scrubland species *Lavandula latifolia*. These only grow well in large masses in alkaline soil.

By nurseryman Jean-Marie Rey
www.jardinerey.fr

Jean-Louis Dumas, director of the fashion house of Hermès, as quoted by Françoise Dorléans in her book *Jardins de la Mode.*

Nicole de Vésian was chic personified…in Bonnieux, under the guidance of her magic fingers, appeared a paradise of southern plants and stones of the Luberon. Nicole, I can still see your small handwritten notes left each morning on my desk on brown paper, each idea expressed in just a few words, starting usually with some version of a triangle. This basic approach, this habit of mind solidly balanced on three geometric points, gave birth each time to some elegant, harmonious project…

Marc Nucera, tree sculptor trained partly by Nicole de Vésian.

In her gardens you find an extreme subtlety in the association of volumes, in the play of colors and tones, that I find in no one else's work, in no other garden. Her tapestries, waves, and plant patchworks have a softly rounded look, so much so that you feel like rolling around in them. She was so successful in creating that sense of gentle refinement, although she herself was not always gentle!

GARDENING FRIENDS

Ione Tézé, already a friend in Paris and owner of the Nogant gardens in Bonnieux.

Each plant, each stone at La Louve has its own story. Some were collected by Nicole on a mountain roadside or in the garden of a friend (who was the donor). For example, all the giant boxwood, were initially given as cuttings only twenty centimeters high by her cousin in Sivergues. Some roses, such as 'Albertine', came from my garden. La Louve, for her close circle who followed each stage of its creation, was the heart of a whole web of friends and supporters, all drawn by the exceptional personality of Nicole.

Scott Stover, friend of Nicole's from the 1980s and partner of Alain David Idoux, owner of La Chabaude, a garden which Nicole helped design in its early stages.

La Louve is a garden for year round living. Nicole never said, "Come in such and such a month to see this or that flower." In every season, this garden, an outdoor room if you wish, a link between the inside and the landscape beyond, was very satisfying to the soul. We were all brought up on the English model of mixed borders, the summer orchestration of floral display. Nicole refused all that, she wanted a garden that would nourish the soul and spirit year round.

Arnaud Maurières and Eric Ossart, designers

La Louve... was Nicole. She was inseparable from her plants and stones. We used to enjoy staying overnight at La Louve. This was not a garden to visit but a garden to live in. We liked her mischievous smile when she wanted to make us believe that a plant had been killed by winter cold when in fact she had thrown it away because she didn't like it in flower. But already, when she died, she had put La Louve behind her. She had a need for new gardening adventures, and was beginning to feel a bit hemmed in by her valley. She dreamed of broad spaces to conquer and a view onto infinity. It is this dream that today moves us the most.

Jean-Marie Rey, nurseryman

Nicole came several times to spend a few days at my place to pick up suitable dry garden plants (phlomis, germanders, etc.) We filled up her car, which was a bit the worse for wear. Her driving was at best artistic. It was Nicole who first gave me the idea of a provençal Zen garden using only olive stumps and creeping rosemaries, to recount in miniature the travels of Odysseus (the myth part was my idea!). She taught me how to remove and reduce, to equate beauty and simplicity.

TWO JOURNALISTS

Daniel H. Minassian, "Provenza dolce e austera".

Solar, infinitely; essential, extreme, insistent, daring extreme purity, extreme sobriety, almost austerity; rigorous as well as creative, inventive and breathing humor, fantasy […] Nicole is, like her house in Bonnieux, one of those beings who leave their mark, their taste, the force of their ideas, not in any facile seductive mode but subtly, with discretion.

Tania Compton, *House and Garden* (in a letter dated 18 March, 1995)

Before visiting La Louve I had never been to a garden which fills one with equal measures of excitement and repose, or that seems to spring so naturally from the earth beneath it whilst keeping you aware of the art, labor and love that has created it. You have achieved such harmony between the improbable contrast of tailor-tight clipping and natural landscape, and miraculously a garden that is radical but perfectly attuned to the countryside that inspired it. Oh, for a grain of your discipline and focus…!

TWO HISTORIANS

John Brookes, *The New Garden: How to design, build and plant your garden with nature in mind*

Perched high in the Luberon hills of southern France is a natural garden *par excellence*, created by the late Nicole de Vésian […] The garden deliberately emphasizes the shapes and textures of this tough region, and the result is surprisingly modern while remaining true to its location. Much of what we find here is both decorative and functional. Bushy herbs such as sage, thyme, rosemary, savory, and cotton lavender are planted close together to provide a wonderful array of greens and greys; planted like this, they also conserve precious moisture. Clipping enables the gardener to explore a range of interesting shapes; but this is also mistral country, and keeping the plants tight prevents the strong winds from tearing them apart.

Sir Roy Strong, in *Ornament in the Small Garden*

It is not often that I bestow the word masterpiece on a garden, but that is an accurate description of this creation by the great French garden designer Nicole de Vésian, who died in 1996. It is the garden she lovingly created around her own house, La Louve, in Provence, which is now cherished and immaculately maintained by the present owner.

Dear Louisa,

Your warm and generous friendship gives me "wings"[...] what can I say in answer to the wonderful images you sent me today? "A shock of joy and emotion", a joy that even makes me take up my pen! The better to thank you with. Thank you for your listening ear, for the generosity of your heart—and of your eye—for the timely friendship which helps light my road so encumbered at the moment with administrative emergencies and 'dictats'. I am hanging on though. Pepped up and encouraged by your friendship and by your stimulating messages that are for me like Reflecting Mirrors...

See you soon,

  With affection,

  Nicole de Vésian

LETTER SENT TO LOUISA JONES
17 JUNE 1996 (SIC)

BOOKS AND ARTICLES CITED

Minassian Daniel H., "Provenza dolce e austera", text and photographs, *AD Italia*, 1990.

Jones Louisa, *Splendeur des jardins de Provence/Gardens in Provence*. Photographs by Vincent Motte and Louisa Jones (Flammarion, 1992).

Osler Mirabel, "Cerebral gardens", *Secret Gardens of France* (Pavilion Books, 1993).

Russell Vivian, "Purist Gardens." *Gardens of the Riviera* (Little Brown and Co, 1993). La Louve appears in the chapter on "Purist Gardens." The same author wrote an article on La Louve for the magazine *Gardens Illustrated.*

"France's Greatest Gardener", *W Magazine*, English edition June-July 1994, interview with William Middleton, photographs by Jacques Dirand.

Compton Tania, "Precious Stones", *House and Garden*, November 1995. Photographs by Kevin Griffen.

Griswold Mac, "A Force of Nature", *Town and Country*, 1995. Photographs by Erica Lennard.

Walden Sarah, *Living in Provence*. Photographs by Solvi dos Santos (Conran Octopus, 1996).

Lovatt-Smith Lisa, *Provence Interiors* (Taschen, 1996).

Pigeat Jean-Paul, *L'Esprit du Japon dans nos jardins* (Ulmer, 2006).

Hill Penelope, *Contemporary History of Garden Design. European Gardens between Art and Architecture* (Birkhauser, 1997).

Jones Louisa, *L'Express Magazine*, 1997. Special issue devoted to Issey Miyake.

Brookes John, *The New Garden : How to design, build and plant your garden with nature in mind* (Dorling Kindersley, 1998).

Jones Louisa, *L'Esprit nouveau des jardins*. Photographs by Vincent Motte (Hachette, 1998).

Jones Louisa, "Clipped Greenery in Provence: the Garden of Nicole de Vésian", *New Zealand Gardener*, 1999.

Dorléans Françoise, *The French Country Garden/Nouveaux jardins de campagne*. Photographs by Gilles Lescanff and Joëlle Mayer (Thames and Hudson, 2000).

Dorléans Françoise, *Jardins de la Mode*. Photographs by Claire de Virieu (Editions du Chêne, 2000).

Seeling Charlotte, *Women and their Gardens/Frauen und ihre Gärten*. Photographs by Corinne Korda and Carina Landau (Gerstenberg Verlag, 2008).

The book on Japanese gardens annotated by Nicole and found in her library by Judith Pillsbury was *A Japanese Touch for your Garden* by Koysohi Seike, Massan Obu Kudo and David H. Engel (Kodansha International, Tokyo-New York-London).

ACKNOWLEDGEMENTS

I must begin by thanking Nicole de Vésian herself. Like many others, I benefitted greatly from her gentle and generous tutorage. I am grateful to the many people close to her who helped me with this book, especially Ghislaine Buisson, Hubert de Vésian, Marc Nucera, Ione Tézé, Devon Fredericks, Scott Stover, Frankie Coxe, Michèle Wachter, Jean-Claude Appy, Arnaud Maurières and Pascale Mussard… A thought also for the many gardeners still working in the Luberon who speak of Nicole de Vésian with reverence and affection. I must warmly thank Judith Pillsbury for giving new life to La Louve and promoting the gardens with enthusiasm and efficiency. How can I thank enough Christian Lacroix for the verve and intelligence of his moving preface, and Jean-Marie Rey, my long-time gardening friend, who adds here his voice as a passionate plantsman. Thanks also to all the many people who helped produce this particularly challenging book, which has involved testimonials and images from so many different sources and periods. And finally, I would like to dedicate this book to my old friend and first photographer Vincent Motte, so sadly no longer with us. He was a true poet of light and a man of exceptional sensitivity.

CRÉDITS PHOTOGRAPHIQUES

Archives : 21, 22 (2), 25 (2)
Ghislaine Buisson : 33
Louisa Jones : 23, 26, 27, 29, 32, 38, 42, 43, 51, 52, 54, 56, 58, 59, 64-65, 68, 69, 72, 73, 74-75 (nos 1, 2 et 3), 76, 82-83 (nos 2 et 3), 84, 88-89, 95, 96, 104-105, 108, 116-117 (nos 1 et 3), 120, 126-127 (nos 2 et 3), 129, 136, 154
Michael Likierman : 30
Vincent Motte : 4, 8, 46-47, 50, 55, 60-61, 94 (et 1re de couverture), 97, 100, 106 (3), 107, 109, 110, 116 (n° 2), 121, 124, 125, 126, 128, 132, 142, 157
Clive Nichols : 14-15, 37, 44, 45 (et 4e de couverture), 48, 53, 62, 63 (2), 66, 70, 77, 78, 79-80, 82 (n° 1), 86, 87, 90, 91, 98-99, 102, 103, 112-113, 114, 118, 122-123, 130, 131, 134-135, 138-139
Matthew Pillsbury : 92-93
Douglas Reed : 34

Achevé d'imprimer en octobre 2012
par l'imprimerie Gibert Clarey Imprimeurs, à Chambray-lès-Tours
pour le compte des éditions Actes Sud
Le Méjan, place Nina-Berberova,
13200 Arles

Suivi éditorial : Aïté Bresson
Conception graphique : Anne-Laure Exbrayat
Fabrication : Géraldine Lay
Photogravure : Terre Neuve

ISBN : 978-2-7427-9734-9
Dépôt légal : avril 2011